GRAND CANYON NATIONAL PARK

A TRUE BOOK

by

David Petersen

CP

Children's Press®
A Division of Grolier Publishing

New York London Hong Kong Sydney

A rabbit in the Grand Canyon

Visit Children's Press® on the Internet at: http://publishing.grolier.com

Library of Congress Cataloging-in-Publication Data

Petersen, David, 1946–
    Grand Canyon National Park / by David Petersen.
        p. cm. — (A true book)
    Includes bibliographical references and index.
    ISBN 0-516-21664-3 (lib. bdg.)   0-516-27316-7 (pbk.)
    1. Grand Canyon National Park (Ariz.)—Juvenile literature. [1. Grand
Canyon National Park (Ariz.) 2. National parks and reserves.] I. Title.
II. Series.
F788 .P48 2001
                                                        979.1'32—dc21
                                                        00-030694

Contents

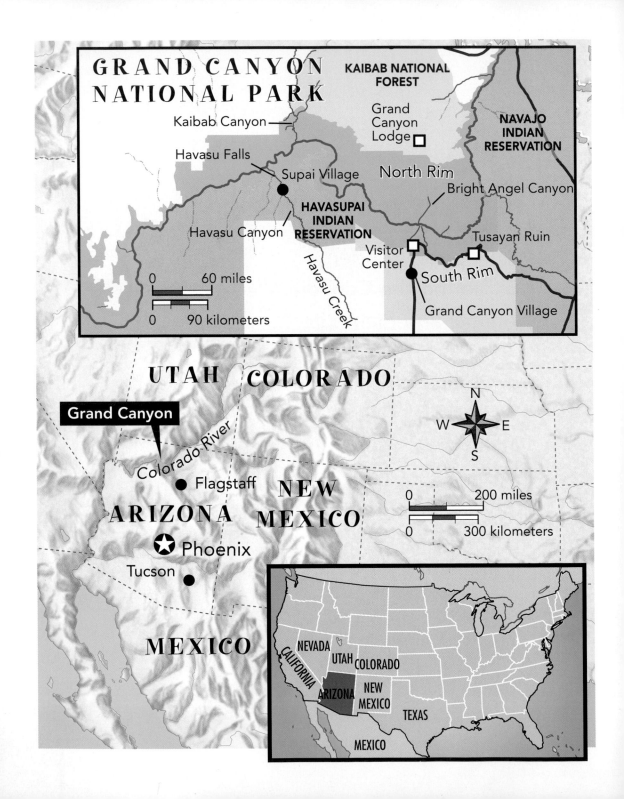

GRAND CANYON
NATIONAL PARK

KAIBAB NATIONAL
FOREST

Kaibab Canyon

Grand
Canyon
Lodge

NAVAJO
INDIAN
RESERVATION

Havasu Falls

Supai Village

North Rim

Bright Angel Canyon

Havasu Canyon

HAVASUPAI
INDIAN
RESERVATION

Tusayan Ruin

Visitor
Center

South Rim

Havasu Creek

0   60 miles

0   90 kilometers

Grand Canyon Village

UTAH   COLORADO

Grand Canyon

Colorado River

N
W   E
S

Flagstaff

NEW
MEXICO

ARIZONA

0   200 miles

0   300 kilometers

Phoenix

Tucson

MEXICO

NEVADA   UTAH COLORADO

CALIFORNIA

ARIZONA   NEW
MEXICO

TEXAS

MEXICO

A Natural Wonder

If you could travel the whole world over, in search of Earth's greatest natural wonders, what might you find? In South America, you could dip a toe into the world's biggest river, the Amazon. In Africa, you could take a camel ride in the world's largest hot desert, the

Sahara. In Asia, you could climb the highest peak on Earth, Mount Everest.

However, the grandest world wonder of them all is right here in North America. It's Grand Canyon, in north-western Arizona. Just how "grand" is this canyon? The word grand can mean big or excellent—the Grand Canyon is both.

The canyon is big and breathtaking. It is 277 miles

A view of the Grand Canyon from the South Rim

(446 kilometers) long, an average of 10 miles (16 km) across, and 1 mile (1.6 km) deep. The canyon is a brilliant rainbow of different colors of rock. It is steep and deep

enough to make you dizzy, rugged and mysterious as the moon, and awesome in its beauty.

The Grand Canyon is a national treasure. Recognizing this, in 1908, President Theodore Roosevelt created a national monument around the canyon to honor and protect it. In 1919, Congress expanded that monument to a park. Today, Grand Canyon National Park includes 1,904

President Theodore Roosevelt at Grand Canyon

square miles (4,931 square kilometers) of natural and human history.

Exploring the Canyon

At Grand Canyon, like nowhere else on Earth, you can see and touch Earth's hidden history. Our planet is about five billion years old—far too vast a time even to imagine. Yet, a record of almost half that time, about two billion years, is exposed in the layered rocks of the canyon walls.

Each layer of rock tells a story about the canyon's history.

Each layer of rock exposed in Grand Canyon's walls represents a different period in Earth's ancient history. The limestone layers were deposited by prehistoric shallow

Limestone, sandstone, and shale can be found in the canyon's walls.

seas. Sandstone layers were formed by long-ago deserts and wind-blown dunes. The shale, or dark, soft, oily rock, tells a tale of muddy river flats, called deltas.

The deepest and oldest rock exposed in the canyon contains little evidence of life. Moving up the canyon walls, and forward in time, fossil remains of simple sea creatures appear. Higher yet are fossil plants, insects, fish, reptiles, and more.

A fossil of a fern plant

The primary tool nature used to carve out this huge, ancient slice of Earth was running water. For millions of years, the mighty Colorado River has roared down from the Rocky Mountains to the east, carrying millions of tons of melted snow to the Gulf of California. And suspended in all that raging water, giving the river its cutting power, are billions of gritty fragments of sand and powdered rock, called silt.

The mighty
Colorado River

Along with sand and silt, the
thundering Colorado River can
move rocks as big as dump
trucks, slamming them against
its bed and banks like giant

battering rams. For some six million years, the Colorado River has bashed, gouged, and ground its way ever deeper into the Colorado Plateau, slicing down through layer upon layer of rock and time.

As the river carves the canyon deeper, other tools of erosion—rain, wind, ice, and gravity—work to widen the canyon, especially near its top edges, or rims. Flash floods create and widen many side canyons. All of these natural

The Colorado
River helps
shape the
Grand Canyon.

forces help shape the park
into the weird, beautiful place
we know today.

Animal and Plant Life

Grand Canyon National Park bustles with life. The park's three distinct life zones, or plant and animal communities, are home to 300 kinds of birds, 88 species of mammals, 58 types of reptiles, and 25 varieties of fish. These three

The Grand Canyon is filled with many different types of plants and animals.

separate habitats are determined by elevation, temperature, and moisture level.

Lowest, hottest, driest, and harshest is the canyon itself. On summer days, air temperatures in the inner gorge average well over 100 degrees Fahrenheit (38 degrees Centigrade). The sun-baked rock is even hotter— almost too hot to touch. Without the Colorado River, little life could survive down there.

The Colorado is a ribbon of life. Along its sandy wet banks grow cottonwoods, willows, and other water-loving, shade-making trees. The shade cools

Trees growing by the Colorado River

the air, slowing evaporation and helping to retain soil moisture. In such happy conditions, many types of plants take root and thrive. In turn, this plant-filled area provides food and shelter from the heat for many animals.

Most canyon animals are small. However, a few large mammals can be found. The desert bighorn sheep loves to walk on the canyon cliffs. The mule deer also calls the park home. Both sheep and deer are herbivores, or plant eaters.

Another group of animals—the carnivores, or meat-eaters—hunt herbivores for food. The largest carnivore in the park is

(Clockwise from top) desert bighorn sheep, a mule deer, and a mountain lion

the mountain lion. This big, graceful cat can be found wherever deer are plentiful, but is very shy and rarely seen.

A pinyon and juniper
forest at the South Rim

Because it is higher, cooler,
and moister than the rocky
canyon bottom, the South Rim
is home to enchanted forests of

pinyon and ponderosa pines and junipers, along with a splendid variety of flowering bushes, cactus, and dry-land wildflowers. Frequently seen South Rim animals include rabbits, squirrels, porcupines, coyotes, and a sky full of birds. Deer are more plentiful here than anywhere else in the park.

Across the canyon, the higher North Rim is the coolest, greenest, and least-crowded part of the park. Here grow dense forests of ponderosa pine, aspen, and other mountain trees. Mirrored lakes, splashing creeks, and flowery meadows make the North Rim a summer paradise for animals and people. The North Rim is open to visitors spring through fall, but deep snow closes the access road every winter.

In this high, lush life zone live some of the park's most interesting creatures. Largest is the elk, a member of the

A family prepares to hike at the North Rim.

deer family. Every autumn, male elk fill the air with their loud, bugle-like mating calls.

27

An elk (above) and a black bear (right)

If you are lucky, you might even catch a glimpse of a big fat black bear, nibbling grass and wildflowers.

The Kaibab Squirrel

The Kaibab squirrel, native to the North Rim of Grand Canyon, is found nowhere else on Earth. It's a large, handsome tree dweller with big ears that are "tasseled" on top with long feathery hairs. Its body is dark, almost black. Its tail is as long as its body, bushy, and white. Often, the Kaibab squirrel will sit in a ponderosa pine, where it lives, its tail wrapped up over its back and head like an umbrella.

The First People

Prehistoric American Indians probably discovered Grand Canyon at least ten thousand years ago. These nomadic hunters and gatherers built no permanent houses, and left little evidence of their passing. The few items left behind are fascinating—small animal dolls,

Prehistoric American Indians made these animal figures around four thousand years ago.

made of split willow twigs twisted together in the shapes of deer and sheep. These four thousand-year-old figurines were not toys, but sacred objects.

People best known today as Anasazi—a Navajo word meaning The Ancient Ones or Ancient Enemies—came to the canyon about one thousand years ago. At first, they too lived by hunting and gathering. Because they wove lovely baskets from yucca and other local desert plants, we call them Basketmakers.

Later, these ancient people learned to grow vegetables for food, and cotton for clothing.

A yucca plant

The ruins of an
Anasazi home
at Tusayan Ruin

They built great apartments of stone, and made fine painted pottery. At Tusayan Ruin, on the South Rim, you can explore the ruins of an eight hundred-year-old Anasazi home.

Not until 1540 did Europeans "discover" Grand Canyon. That year, guided by Hopi Indian scouts, the Spanish explorer Garcia Lopez de Cardeñas became the first European to peer into the great gaping gorge.

Living in the Canyon Today

The Havasupai—"People of the Blue-Green Water"—call the canyon their home. Their American Indian reservation is located in the southwest corner of the park. In Supai Village, the Havasupai tend livestock, grow gardens, and sell goods and services to visitors. Other

Supai Village (above); Havasupai kids playing basketball (left)

native peoples living near the park include the Navajo, Hualapai, Hopi, and Kaibab-Paiute tribes.

Near Supai Village, hidden in a narrow, tree-shaded side canyon, is the place from which the Havasupai take their tribal name. Here, lively Havasu Creek tumbles over a ledge to form roaring Havasu Falls. At the base of the falls lies a large and lovely pool of sparkling blue-green water.

Havasu Falls

Visiting the Grand Canyon

Millions of people from all around the world come to explore the grandest canyon on Earth every year. There are many ways to see and enjoy this gigantic park—including by automobile, tour bus, antique railroad train, mule train, and river raft.

Exploring the canyon by mule and by boat

However, one of the best ways to see the park is to take a hike. The park offers 400 miles (644 km) of scenic hiking trails, running along both rims and down into the canyon. All you need are good

A mother and son hike in the park.

hiking shoes, a sun hat, snacks, lots of water, and a thirst for adventure.

No matter how you choose to explore it, Grand Canyon National Park, in Arizona, is a great place to begin your personal search for Earth's greatest natural wonders.

Fast Facts

Location: northwestern Arizona, U.S.A.

Nearest city: Flagstaff, Arizona

Established: 1919

Size of park: 1,904 square miles (4,931 sq. km)

Age of canyon: about 6 million years

Length of canyon: 277 miles (446 km)

Depth of canyon: 4,500 feet (1,372 meters) at South Rim; 5,700 feet (1,737 m) at North Rim; 1 mile (1.6 km) average

Width of canyon between rims: 10 miles (16 km) average; greatest width 18 miles (29 km)

Distances from South to North Rim: 12 miles (19 km) straight-line; 21 miles (34 km) by trail; 215 miles (346 km) by road

Height: North Rim 8,000 feet (2,438 m) above sea level; South Rim average 6,800 feet (2,072 m) above sea level; Colorado River 2,200 feet (670 m) above sea level

Annual rainfall: South Rim average 16 inches (41 centimeters); North Rim 26 inches (66 cm)

To Find Out More

Here are some additional resources to help you learn more about Grand Canyon National Park and Arizona:

 **Books**

Anderson, Peter. **A Grand Canyon Journey.** Franklin Watts, 1997.

Fradin, Dennis Brindell. **Arizona.** Children's Press, 1994.

Our National Parks. The Reader's Digest Association, 1985.

Rawlins, Carol. **The Grand Canyon.** Raintree Steck-Vaughn, 1995.

Organizations and Online Sites

**Grand Canyon
National Park**
P.O. Box 129
Grand Canyon, AZ 86023

Grand Canyon Association
P.O. Box 399
Grand Canyon, AZ 86023

**Great Outdoor
Recreation Pages**
http://www.gorp.com

Learn more about hiking
and other outdoor activi-
ties at U.S. national parks
and other places around
the world.

National Park Service
http://www.nps.gov/

This site offers official infor-
mation on the National
Park Service, with links to
many national park and
monument sites.

Touring Grand Canyon
http://www.thecanyon.com

This site provides a photo
gallery so that you get a
glimpse of the Grand
Canyon and learn more
about visiting the park.

Important Words

elevation height above sea level

erosion the slow wearing away of rock or other material by water, wind, ice, and other natural forces

evaporation the conversion by heat of liquid to vapor, as when boiling water becomes steam

fossil the ancient, stony remains of plants and animals; fossils can be an organism's body, or merely a track or imprint

mammals animals that are born live (rather than hatched from eggs), nurse their mother's milk as infants, and are usually covered with hair; humans are mammals

nomadic constantly moving

Index

Meet the Author

David Petersen lives with one wife and two dogs in a little cabin on a big mountain in Colorado. David loves exploring and writing about Grand Canyon and other national parks and monuments. David also writes "big kid's" books about nature, most recently including *Elkheart: A Personal Tribute to Wapiti and Their World* (Boulder, Colo., Johnson Books, 1998).

Photographs ©: Dembinsky Photo Assoc.: 1 (Darrell Gulin), 19 (Martin Withers/FRPS); Grand Canyon National Park: 9 (#5556); Liaison Agency, Inc.: 41 bottom (Richard Elkins), 33, 41 top (G. Brad Lewis), 39 (Mark Lewis), 2 (Brad Markel), 11 (Steven Burr Williams); Photo Researchers: 23 right (Jerry L. Ferrara), 28 right, 29 (Pat & Tom Leeson), 23 bottom left (Jeff Lepore); Stone: 15 (John Beatty), cover (Bob Thomason); Tom Bean: 7, 12, 13, 17, 24, 27, 31, 37 bottom, 37 top, 42, 43; Visuals Unlimited: 34 (Bob Clay), 23 top left (Jeff Greenberg), 28 left (Leonard Lee Rue III), 21 (Kjell B. Sandved).

Map by Joe LeMonnier